Series editor:
W. Owen Cole

The
Qur'an

Ruqaiyyah Waris Maqsood

HEINEMANN

Heinemann Educational
a division of Heinemann Publishers (Oxford) Ltd
Halley Court, Jordan Hill, Oxford OX2 8EJ

OXFORD LONDON EDINBURGH
MADRID ATHENS BOLOGNA PARIS
MELBOURNE SYDNEY AUCKLAND
SINGAPORE TOKYO IBADAN NAIROBI
HARARE GABORONE PORTSMOUTH NH (USA)

© Ruqaiyyah Waris Maqsood 1993

First published 1993

**A catalogue record for this book is
available from the British Library**

ISBN 0 435 30352 X

94 95 96 97 10 9 8 7 6 5 4 3 2

Designed and produced by Visual Image, Street

Cover design by Philip Parkhouse, Abingdon

Produced by Mandarin Offset
Printed and bound in China

Introduction to the series

The purpose of these books is to show what the scriptures of the six religions in the series are, to tell the story of how they grew into their present form, and to give some idea of how they are used and what they mean to believers. It is hoped that readers will be able to appreciate how important the sacred texts are to those who base their lives on them and use them to develop their faith as well as their knowledge. For this reason, members of the six major religions found in Britain today have been asked to write these books.

W. Owen Cole (Series Editor)

Acknowledgements

Thanks are due to Imam Rahmat Aziz Salik of the Hull Mosque for his kind help and encouragement with the text; and to my librarians Trevor Norman and Gwyneth Major for helping with my research over the years. Thanks also to my husband Waris Ali Maqsood for putting up with harassment, and to all those who kindly allowed me to photograph them, especially Maysoon and Hoger Akrawi and their children Lara and Tara; and my friends Waheed, Ruhul, Abdul Ghafur al-Heeti, Kashim, Norhana, Zafer and his son Yusuf, Muhammad Rehouma, Abdul Karim and Vincent Dourthe, and the Imam's son Zia-ur-Rahman.

The Publishers would like to thank the following for permission to reproduce photographs:

Tim Butcher p.30; Nasjonalgalleriet, Oslo/Bridgeman Art Library p.26; Royal Observatory, Edinburgh/Science Photo Library p.36; Peter Sanders pp.4, 5, 6, 8, 15, 16, 20, 22, 24, 25, 31, 34, 37, 42, 44.

Cover photographs by Peter Sanders.

All other photographs supplied by the author.

Contents

1 The life of Muhammad

This section tells you about the early life of the Prophet Muhammad, and his call to be the Prophet of Islam.

Muhammad was an Arab of the Hashem clan in the Quraish tribe. He was born in Makkah in about 570CE. He never knew his father, Abdullah, who died before he was born, and his mother, Amina, died when he was only six years old, leaving him an orphan. He was brought up by his grandfather, a devout and wise tribal leader, and then by his uncle Abu Talib, a wealthy merchant.

As a youth, Muhammad worked as a shepherd, and later helped his uncle on trade expeditions. He became well known for his outstanding honesty, kindness, wisdom and fair dealings, and was noticed by the wealthy widow Khadijah, who employed him to look after her merchant business for her. They respected each other, and this respect turned to love, even though Khadijah was about 40 years old and Muhammad was 25. They got married and lived very happily together for about 25 years, until Khadijah died. They had six children – four girls and two boys – but unfortunately, both the boys died while very young. When his uncle Abu Talib fell on hard times, Muhammad took his little son Ali into his household, and he also brought up a slave boy, Zaid, as his own son.

Muhammad grew up in a period of great corruption, when the Arab tribes worshipped many idols in the ancient temple of Makkah, known as the Ka'ba. Many religious people did not really believe that there were lots of gods, or that objects made of stone and wood had any power at all; they regarded this sort of thing as superstition, and believed that there was really only one true god. Muhammad was one of these people, known by the Arabs as hanifs. Other people believed in all the 'gods' in the Ka'ba, and thought that if they neglected or upset them, they had the power to spoil the harvest or cause drought and sickness.

Muhammad's call

Muhammad frequently went off by himself to pray and think, sometimes staying on the nearby hillsides for days. One night he had a vision of an **angel**, a being who identified himself as Gabriel, God's chief messenger. Gabriel assured him that there was only one god, called Allah, and brought him a **revelation** from Him. Muhammad was very frightened, and did not know if he was going mad, or if he had seen an evil spirit; but when he went home, Khadijah listened to his story and was convinced that this was a genuine message from Allah, and that Muhammad had been called to be a **prophet**.

The Prophet Muhammad worked as a shepherd on the hills around Makkah.

Muhammad was not the first prophet. Allah had called many people in the past to be His messengers: the last prophet before Muhammad was the Blessed Jesus of Nazareth. Muhammad was told that he had to 'rise and warn' the people around him, for their lives were corrupt and full of sin, and they thought that if they just made **sacrifices** to the idols, it did not matter what else they did, or whether they were bad people. They did not realize that there was a life to come after death, in which they would be rewarded or punished according to how they had lived on earth. It was Muhammad's duty to tell as many people as possible, and to record with perfect accuracy the messages revealed to him by Allah, so that the revelation would be available to all people, even after he had died.

During the next 23 years, Muhammad did just this. By the time he died, in 632CE, a

The Ka'ba temple in Makkah, the 'centre' of Islam. Muslims believe it stands on the foundations of the oldest shrine of God on earth.

holy book consisting of the collection of all these revelations had been put together and carefully checked. This book was the Holy Qur'an.

NEW WORDS

Angel a special type of being created by God to act as a messenger

Prophet a person who receives a message from God

Revelation a message sent from God to a human mind

Sacrifice giving something to God (this gift was usually the life of an animal) or going without something you value for the sake of God

FOR DISCUSSION

1 Why do you think Allah might have thought Muhammad was a good choice to be one of His messengers?

2 Explain why some people thought it was dangerous not to worship the idols. How do you think these people would react if anyone tried to stop them?

3 'You have indeed in the messenger of Allah a beautiful pattern for anyone who believes in God and the Life to Come, and who lives in praise of God.' (Surah 33:21.) In what ways was Muhammad's life already a 'beautiful pattern' for future believers?

THINGS TO DO

1 Imagine you are one of the people who knew Muhammad. Write a letter to a friend telling what happened when Muhammad came down from the hillside. How did you feel about what he told you? How do you think the people of Makkah are going to react?

2 The first revelations

This section tells you how Muhammad began his ministry, and what his early message was.

When Muhammad began telling people about what had happened to him, and explaining what the revealed messages were, most people did not believe him at first. He had lived up to the age of 40 without having anything like this happen to him before; everyone knew he was a good and kind man, but they knew him as a merchant and a wealthy trader. They found it difficult to see him suddenly in a different way.

Muhammad told them about his first vision. The night on which it happened is known as the '**Lailat ul Qadr**', or 'Night of Power'.

Muhammad was alone on the mountain when he heard a voice calling his name and ordering him to 'recite'. He saw some letters appear which looked as if they were made of fire, but he could not read what they said. Although Muhammad was a merchant, he was not an educated man, and the Qur'an calls him 'unlettered' several times (e.g. Surah 7:157). This may have meant that he could not even read.

Muhammad's instructions

The voice commanded him three times, and then he felt something grip his body and throat, and he thought he was going to die. Suddenly, he knew what the words said, and began to recite them. The words began:

'In the name of your Lord, who created all humanity from an original droplet, speak these words out loud! Your Lord is the Most Generous One – He who has taught the Pen, and taught humans what they did not know.'

(Surah 96:1–5.)

Mt. Hira near Makkah. The Prophet Muhammad used to come here alone, to pray and think.

The revelation went on to warn human beings not to live bad lives, but to give up their selfishness and corruption. They were not aware that there was any god watching them who would make them pay one day for the things they did wrong, but Allah saw everything. Muhammad was told to pay no attention to them, but to bring himself closer to Allah in his life (96:19). He was to be brave, and to speak out, no matter what other people said or did to him. He was to give everybody the chance to think seriously about the way they were living, and do something about it before it was too late. He was told that his message was really nothing new – there had been plenty of other messengers before him who had taught the truths about God, but people did not want to listen. They wanted to carry on doing wicked and selfish things, and did not care how much they hurt others, so long as they got what they wanted.

Muhammad was to tell them that all these things they wanted so desperately – things like money and big houses and fancy clothes and jewellery, and beautiful faces and figures – were not the real things that mattered. Some of the ways in which they liked to spend their time were making their characters go bad. Muhammad's message was intended to make them think again about whether they were doing right or wrong, or being sensible or stupid.

Many people did not believe him, but some of the revelations in the Qur'an supported him personally, and defended his claims.

NEW WORDS

Lailat ul Qadr the Night of Power: the night when Muhammad first received a revelation from Allah

Missionary somebody sent out by God to do His work and tell people about Him.

'O people! Your companion is not one possessed. He saw him [Gabriel] without any doubt in the clear horizon; he keeps nothing back of what was revealed to him; it is not the word of an evil spirit.' (Surah 81:22–25.)

'By the star when it sets! Your fellow man (Muhammad) is not making a mistake, and he has not been misled. He is not speaking from mere impulse. The Qur'an is nothing less than that which was revealed to him. One mighty in power showed it to him, one full of wisdom. He revealed to His servant what He revealed. The servant did not make false in his heart anything that he saw.'

(Surah 43:1–11.)

FOR DISCUSSION

1 Explain why you think many people did not believe Muhammad at first.

2 What difficulties do you think you would have if you were suddenly called upon to change your life and become a **missionary**? How do you think your own family and the people in your town would react?

THINGS TO DO

1 In sentences, give an example of:

   i something selfish;
   ii something corrupt;
   iii something stupid;
   iv something brave.

2 Choose one of the passages from the Qur'an given in this unit and write it out carefully. Draw a colourful or patterned border around it.

3 Put the heading: 'Things the Qur'an taught were wrong'. Draw a series of pictures or cartoons to illustrate:

   i wealth and greed;
   ii selfishness;
   iii getting drunk.

3 Acceptance at Madinah

This section tells you about Muhammad's sufferings, and his eventual success when he moved to Madinah.

Muhammad's first **converts** were his wife Khadijah and the two young boys who lived with them, Ali and Zaid. Most of the members of Muhammad's tribe were very embarrassed, and turned against him. They did not believe what he had to say, and they were particularly angry because they made a lot of money out of the pilgrims who came every year to the shrine at Makkah to worship the idols. They did not want to lose their profits. Muhammad was telling everyone that there was only one God, and that the idols were powerless bits of stone, and it was pointless worshipping them.

Muhammad's uncle Abu Lahab was very angry with him, and stirred up trouble. The kind uncle who had brought Muhammad up, Abu Talib, protected Muhammad, but he did not believe in the Qur'an. When he saw Muhammad and the little boys praying, he laughed at their undignified position, and thought they were being stupid.

Some people did listen to Muhammad, however, and they realized that what he said made a lot of sense. The words of the Holy Qur'an were so powerful and moving that they made people think deeply. Some of the words were very direct, and told people what to do. Other words frightened them, because they warned of what would happen to selfish and wicked people, and they knew they had done lots of wrong things themselves. Whenever people were sorry for what they had done wrong, Muhammad told them Allah would welcome them and forgive them – if they would change their ways and start to live under a new kind of discipline.

People come to Islam

The sort of people who listened to Muhammad and agreed the most were people who had been badly treated, or who had been unfortunate in life: people such as slaves, and women who were unhappy because of the way their menfolk treated them. A lot of

The Quba Mosque in Madinah. The Prophet often came here for prayer and rest.

young people began to take Muhammad seriously, and that made some of the elders angry. They said Muhammad was trying to split up families, and lead people astray, and make them give up the respected traditions of their forefathers.

Muhammad said that he only wanted to bring people closer to Allah – but that sometimes this did mean upsetting other people. Those who believed in the Holy Qur'an had to put Allah before everything and everybody else – even their own families or ancient customs. They had to believe what the Qur'an told them, and agree in their hearts to do what it said. This was called '**submission**' or '**Islam**'. Those who submitted were to be known as Muslims. Men and women were equal Muslims, of equal worth in the eyes of Allah, and of equal responsibility. Nobody would be able to make excuses for anybody else – each person was an individual and had to choose for him or herself.

Changes

Ten years after receiving the first revelation, Muhammad felt very depressed. Two people whom he loved dearly died: his wife Khadijah and his uncle Abu Talib. He tried moving to a town called Taif, but the people there **persecuted** him and laughed at him.

Suddenly, Muhammad was granted another wonderful experience: the '**Lailat ul-Miraj**' or 'Ascent to Paradise'. He was granted a vision of the highest heavens, and his faith was strengthened.

After twelve years of struggling to make converts in Makkah, Muhammad was eventually invited to go to the town of Yathrib and live there as the town's ruler. He agreed to go, and the town became known as Madinat-al-Nabi (the town of the Prophet), or simply Madinah.

FOR DISCUSSION

1 Why do you think that people such as slaves, women and youngsters accepted Muhammad more easily than the rich businessmen?

2 Explain what is meant by the word 'Muslim'. Why were people called this?

3 Muslims never show Muhammad in pictures or include him in plays. Why do you think this is so?

THINGS TO DO

1 Write a short play based on an argument about Muhammad between Muhammad's uncle Abu Lahab, and one of the boys, Ali or Zaid. What do you think they might have said to each other?

2 Draw a picture to illustrate the people of Makkah persecuting the Muslims.

NEW WORDS

Convert someone who starts believing in a new religion

Islam the religion of 'submission to Allah (God)'

Lailat ul-Miraj the night Muhammad had his special 'journey' to Heaven

Persecution being hurt or ridiculed by other people

Submission replacing your own will with someone else's

'Those who God wills to guide, He opens their hearts to Islam.' (Surah 6:125.)

4 Receiving the revelations

This section tells you about the different ways in which Muhammad received the revelations from Allah.

Muhammad was a very successful ruler in Madinah, and while he lived there the rest of the revelations of the Qur'an were given to him. On many occasions Allah spoke to him through the angel Gabriel again. Muhammad described him as being a huge figure, or just a pair of eyes that seemed to watch him from every direction.

Sometimes the message came to Muhammad without any warning, while he was out riding, or teaching the people. Occasionally it was in direct answer to a specific question or problem that had been worrying him. At other times, he fell into a trance-like state, and lay down covered in his cloak. Sometimes he seemed to lose consciousness, or became very hot and soaked with sweat. Sometimes the voice was not at all clear, and he said it felt as if his head was ringing with noises like muffled bells; when this happened, he could not work out what the voice was saying. At other times the voice was very clear, and he could hear the words with no difficulty.

Muhammad was always very affected by the revelations, and sometimes felt as if he was dying. He said: 'Not once did I receive a revelation without thinking that my soul had been torn away.' (**Hadith** – a saying of Muhammad.)

Whatever happened, at the end of the experience Muhammad would go back to normal again, and repeat the message carefully to witnesses, and make them learn it by heart.

Muhammad's words

It is very important to realize that Muhammad never claimed to have written the Qur'an himself. No Muslim believes it to be the work of Muhammad. Many of the sayings and teachings of Muhammad have been recorded and collected up by his followers, and these have quite a different style from the revelations of the Qur'an. Muhammad's own sayings are known as the hadith. The hadith are in the ordinary spoken Arabic of Muhammad's time; the verses in the Qur'an are in a unique and special style that is different from any other book or writing. Muslims believe the Qur'an was the word of Allah, exactly as Muhammad received it. Muhammad was simply the transmitter, the mouth-piece through which the words were revealed to people.

Muhammad faced many people who did not believe that he was a genuine prophet. They challenged him to work a miracle to prove himself. He always said that he was not a miracle-worker, and that the prophet famous for miracles was the Blessed Jesus.

'Give glory to your Guardian Lord, and lift your heart in prayer.' (Surah 87:15.)

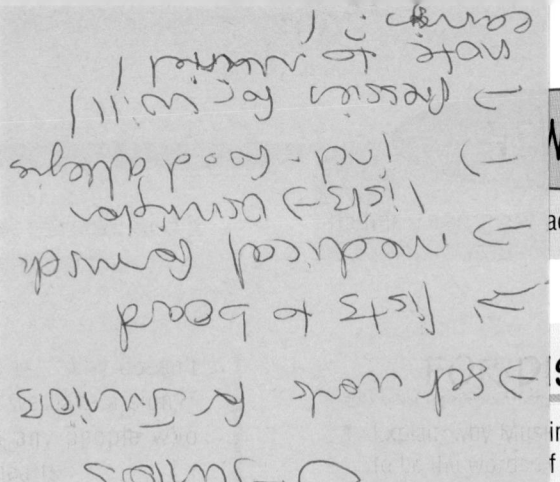

The Qur'an itself was a grea... ...aching of Muhammad's own
was the only miracle necess... ...
followers.

'Those without knowledge ...
God speak to us, why can't ...
But the signs are clear to ... ...ims do not believe the Qur'an
hold firmly to faith in their ... ...f Muhammad himself.

...le ask to see a miracle? Why
...eat this request as a foolish
...one?

Muhammad had absolute confidence in the
message he was passing on. Allah always
reassured him, and vouched for his integrity.
For example, on one occasion Allah said:

'Unbelievers might well stare at you and
abuse you, and call you mad – but you have
nothing less than a message to all the world.'
(Surah 68:52.)

THINGS TO DO

1 Make a list of some of the ways in which
Muhammad received his revelations.

2 Some people suggested that Muhammad had
epilepsy, or was possessed by an evil spirit.
See if you can think of any reasons why this
seems not to be true. Make a list of reasons.
For example, think of the things that
Muhammad was teaching.

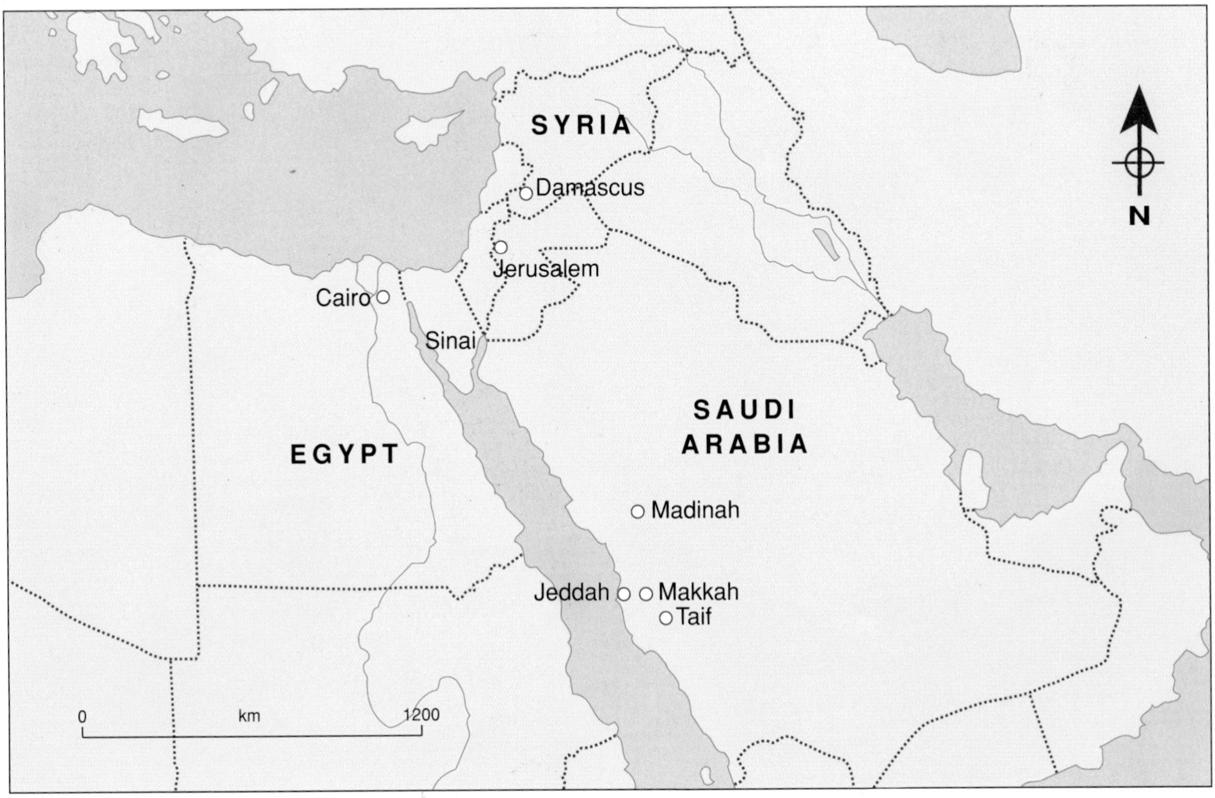

SYRIA

Damascus

Jerusalem

Cairo

Sinai

EGYPT

SAUDI
ARABIA

Madinah

Jeddah Makkah
Taif

N

0   km   1200

5 The Qur'an is completed

This section tells you about the end of Muhammad's life, and how the Qur'an was completed.

In the year 630CE Muhammad was able to go back to Makkah with a huge army of 10,000 men. The Makkans knew that this time they would be defeated. However, instead of fighting them, Muhammad entered Makkah in peace, and called for everyone to come to prayer. He went into the Ka'ba shrine and destroyed all the idols.

Muhammad was a very gentle and kind conqueror, and forgave all those who had fought against him or hurt his followers in the past. Soon everyone in Makkah accepted the faith of Islam, and Makkah was declared a holy city dedicated to Allah. Anyone who was not a Muslim was no longer allowed to enter it.

Muhammad had only another two years to live. Before he died, he made sure that all the revelations of the Qur'an had been properly recorded and learnt.

Single verses of the revelation are known as ayats (**ayah** in the singular), and chapters are called **surahs**. The Qur'an has 114 surahs and 6,616 ayats – a total of 78,000 words.

When the revelation was complete, Allah revealed to Muhammad the order in which He wished the surahs to be arranged. It was not the same order in which they had been given to Muhammad. In fact, when you look at the Qur'an, you could almost say that the

'This Book We have revealed as a blessing; so follow it and be righteous, that you may receive mercy.' (Surah 6:155.)

'When the Qur'an is read, listen to it with attention.' (Surah 7:205.)

The last revelation was probably that of Surah 5:3:

> 'Today I have perfected your religion for you, completed My favour upon you, and have chosen for you Islam as the way of your life.'

The Blessed Prophet Muhammad died on 8 June 632 CE – in the Islamic calendar, this is 12 Rabi'ul-Awwal 11 AH.

> 'If all the waters of the sea were ink with which to write the words of my Lord, the sea would surely be drained before His words are finished, even if we were to add to it sea upon sea.' (Surah 18:109.)

short surahs at the end were the ones that were given first, and that the long ones at the beginning belong to the later period, in Madinah. Muhammad was made to recite the order and learn it, and the angel checked it with him several times before Muhammad died. This is the same order in which the surahs are found in the Qur'an today.

The duty to study

Reading and understanding the Qur'an is the first duty of all Muslims, for it is the guide to their lives. It shows them what Allah is like, and what His qualities and characteristics are.

Some of the verses in the Qur'an are very clear and straightforward, and very simple to understand. Others are more complicated, and are not intended to be taken literally, but need to be interpreted carefully to see what deep meaning is hidden beneath the surface. A person could study the verses for a lifetime, and still find something new every time.

FOR DISCUSSION

1 Explain why Muslims accept the surahs of the Qur'an in the 'wrong' order.

2 Why is the study of the Qur'an the first and most important duty of any Muslim?

THINGS TO DO

1 Copy out the words of Surah 18:109 and make a decorative border around them.

2 a Imagine you are a citizen of Makkah. Write a postcard to a friend describing what happened when Muhammad captured the city, and how things were changed.

 b Draw a picture of the Ka'ba shrine as the 'front' of your postcard.

NEW WORDS

Ayah one verse of the Qur'an

Surah a section of the Qur'an organized as a chapter

6 The exact message

This section tells you about how the Qur'an was put together as a book and preserved in its exact words.

Each time Muhammad received a revelation he learnt it by heart and recited it to other people, and made them learn it by heart, too. This was one simple way in which they could check the accuracy with each other. Some people wrote the revelations down, even though they did not all have paper to write on. They used bits of scraped leather, smooth white stones, pieces of bone (especially shoulder-blades) and even the bleached tough leaves of date palm.

Some people loved the Qur'an so much that they made the effort to learn all of it by heart. They did this by repeating the ayats over and over again. The unusual, poetic and rhythmic style of the revealed words made it easy to learn in this way. Anybody who learnt the whole Qur'an was known as a **hafiz**. Many Muslims to this day have managed to achieve this, and they are all called huffaz (plural). Muslims usually start learning the verses when they are small children. Sometimes Muslims around the world who are not Arabs and cannot speak Arabic still manage to learn the verses by heart; of course, these Muslims also have to find out what the verses mean!

Muslims believe it is very important that the Qur'an is preserved in its exact Arabic words. Whenever anyone makes a translation into a different language, the translator's skill or point of view influences his or her choice of words; it cannot be avoided. The Qur'an in any language other than Arabic is never regarded by Muslims as having the same authority as the original, because it has been interpreted by some human brain. All devout Muslims try to learn Arabic, so that they can understand fully what they are reading – but for some people this is a very difficult task.

Nothing altered

Muslims became worried about how the accuracy of the messages could be checked

'We reveal to you the Truth, and the best explanation of it.' (Surah 25:33.)

after the death of Muhammad. The Prophet's closest friends, Abu Bakr and Umar, advised that the messages should be collected into a book form. Muhammad had a reliable helper, Zaid ibn Thabit, who was given the task of gathering all the revelations together and putting them in the sequence ordered by Muhammad. Zaid did not alter the messages in any way; he did not try to put in explanations or comments, or to write in little bits of information or 'story' to help the reader. He made it his duty to be exact. Nothing was added to the messages, nothing removed and nothing altered.

The Muslims accepted that the special words of the Qur'an were to be kept completely separate from other human words and thoughts, because they were the words of Allah Himself, and He had given the messages exactly as He wished them to be given. Even if people did not understand something, they were not to alter anything – and some of the things in the message were not understood at all until many centuries later! If the words had been tampered with to fit the understanding of that particular time, much of the deep meaning for today's Muslims would have been lost. It was the responsibility of Zaid to make sure that nothing was lost or altered.

Copying the Qur'an

Muhammad remarried several times after the death of Khadijah. His wife Hafsa, who was his friend Umar's daughter, was given this unique book and kept it safe, and later people were able to check their versions against this original. Later the **caliph** Uthman had copies made and sent to all the chief Muslim places. Two of these very early copies still exist today: one in Istanbul and one in Tashkent. Modern technology has now taken over: the Tashkent Qur'an has recently been photocopied.

FOR DISCUSSION

1 Why do Muslims regard it as vitally important to learn the Qur'an in Arabic – the original language?

2 Explain what happens to the original words of any piece of writing when someone translates them into another language.

THINGS TO DO

1 Draw a series of pictures to illustrate the kind of things the Qur'an verses had been preserved on or in.

2 Write a short dialogue between Zaid ibn Thabit and Hafsa discussing what Zaid had done and the importance of his work.

'Here are signs self-evident in the hearts of those blessed with knowledge.' (Surah 29:49.)

7 The unique message

A Qur'an written in beautiful writing.

This section tells you how the Qur'an is different from other holy books.

Muslims hold several beliefs about the Qur'an. First, they claim that it is the only holy book in the world to have survived in exact and unaltered form up to the present day, after 1,400 years. Secondly, they believe it has a very particular and individual style that is impossible to copy, since it is Allah's recorded speech given directly to Muhammad, and not a 'written' document.

The Qur'an states that:

'If the whole of mankind and **jinns** were to gather together to produce the like of this Qur'an, they could not produce anything like it, even if they backed each other up with help and support.' (Surah 17:88.)

People who read the Qur'an without realizing what it is claiming to be, or knowing either its background or how it was put together, are sometimes very critical of its style and point out that it is disjointed, or jumps from one subject to another, and has phrases in it which do not appear to have been composed in the normal manner used by writers. It is important to realize that all these things are true – because of what the Qur'an really is.

You never find a 'story-line' approach in the Qur'an. Any film-maker would have a very difficult job trying to pick out some plot for a religious film from these pages. You never get historical narrative about Muhammad or what was going on at the time – things like: 'Muhammad was in the cave on Mount Hira when...' or 'Muhammad went up

16

to the elders and said...'. You never get details about Muhammad's private life, or about his wives or daughters.

Strangely enough, there are bits in the Qur'an about Muhammad. However, these are always part of the revelation and are part of whatever it was Muhammad was being told to 'say' or 'recite'. For example:

> 'Say: I am but a man like yourselves, but the inspiration has come to me, that your God is One God.'   (Surah 18:110.)

Another unique feature is that the Qur'an does not really have a beginning, middle and end. The first verses of the Qur'an to be revealed were actually Surah 96! The Qur'an is not a 'story' but rather like a computer, giving the answers to whatever question is put to it.

Wise and sympathetic people can argue about the rights and wrongs of things for ages, but the answers given in the Qur'an are usually startlingly precise. For example: how long do you think it would be right for a widow to wait before remarrying? Many major world religions give sensible answers to this; but the Qur'an is precise – four months and ten days (Surah 2:234). The Qur'an is full of examples like this.

Muhammad not a scholar

A further difference about the Qur'an is the way it was revealed through Muhammad. Up to the age of 40, Muhammad had never been known as a teacher, philosopher, scholar, or any kind of expert. He had never travelled anywhere far from the deserts of Arabia or seen anything other than the cities where he had traded. He knew nothing of science, or the scriptures of the Jews or Christians – he was an 'unlearned' man, and there were as yet no copies of the Jewish or Christian holy books in Arabic:

> 'And you, O Muhammad, were not able to recite a book before this [book came], nor are you able to transcribe it with your right hand.'   (Surah 29:48.)

Yet, after the Night of Power, when he received the first revelation, and for the rest of his life, Muhammad continued to receive messages that involved a very comprehensive knowledge of every aspect of the universe, and the hidden spiritual worlds beyond. It also implied a full knowledge of what had been revealed to previous prophets (in Judaism and Christianity) and where the believers in the previous teachings of Allah had 'gone wrong'.

NEW WORD

Jinn a kind of being, neither good nor evil, created by God

FOR DISCUSSION

1 Explain why the revelations in the Qur'an seem to be 'disjointed', or lacking in order.

2 How does the behaviour of Muhammad after the Night of Power suggest that something very extraordinary had happened to him?

THINGS TO DO

1 Which of these statements do Muslims think are true, and which do they think are false? Write out the true ones, then alter the false ones to make them fit in with Muslim beliefs.
   i It would be easy to invent revelations of the Qur'an by copying the style.
   ii The Qur'an gives us the 'story' of Muhammad.
   iii Muhammad was a 'superhuman' being, more than a man.
   iv Muhammad had never studied to be a scholar.

2 You are the editor of a newspaper. Write a short article entitled 'Muhammad – man of mystery', telling about this Arab trader and what happened to him.

This section tells you how the Qur'an is given reverence and used in the daily lives of Muslims.

The act of reciting the Qur'an with soul, heart, mind, tongue and body is known as tilawah. All people reading the Qur'an should find benefit from it, provided they come to it with an open mind. Muslims, however, read it with strong purpose: the desire to find out what Allah wants them to do, and then to change their lives so that they are actively doing it.

It is vital that the Qur'an is read with understanding. Some Muslims claim that the mere act of reading or reciting the Qur'an alone is an act of merit, and some can recite it in Arabic without knowing what it means. This may be a discipline and devotion which earns some reward, but they are not getting the full blessings intended. The Qur'an is not being given the chance to fulfil its purpose.

Muslims should consider each word of the Qur'an as if it has just been revealed to them personally. They will miss the point if what they have read does not alter the quality of

their lives, or if they go on to act in ways which are disapproved of by the Qur'an. Claiming (or pretending) to live the Muslim way of life, but really acting in ways disapproved of by the Qur'an, is known as hypocrisy:

> 'Your actions are worthless if they are not backed up by your beliefs; and your beliefs are worthless if they are not backed up by your actions.' (Hadith.)

It is recommended that the Qur'an is read every day and, in fact, no true Muslim would consider the day complete without it, for it has to be recited during prayers.

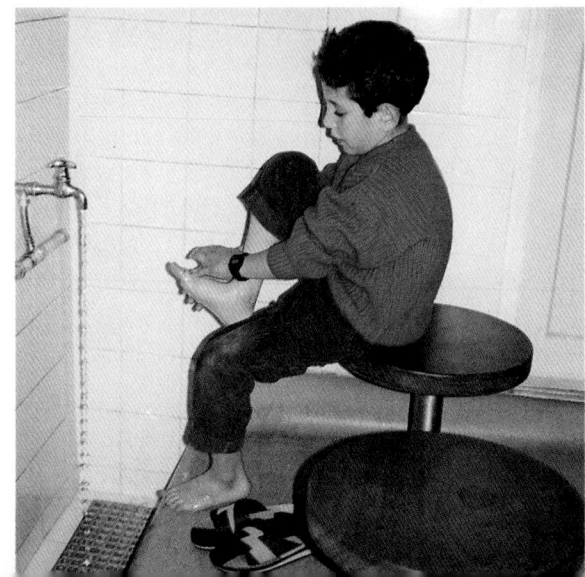

Performing wudu. 'O believers! When you prepare for prayer, wash your faces and your hands (and arms) to the elbows; rub your heads; and your feet to the ankles.' (Surah 5:7.)

Qur'an

Reading the Qur'an

When sitting down to read, Muslims believe it is better to study a small portion than a large section, and to try to gain full understanding. Some of the great Muslims spent days, months and years contemplating just a single verse. There is no merit in claiming to have read through the Qur'an at a very fast speed; Muhammad's companion Umar said that 'one who finished it in less than three days did not understand any of it'.

Before starting to recite, Muslims need to be in a state of ritual cleanliness, or **wudu**. This involves washing certain parts of the body, and, if possible, wearing clean clothes and standing or sitting in a clean place:

'When you prepare for prayer (or for reading the Qur'an) wash your faces and your hands (and arms) up to the elbows; rub your heads with water, and your feet to the ankles. If you are in a state of impurity bathe your whole body.... If you find no water, then take for yourselves clean sand or earth and rub your faces and hands with it. Allah does not wish to place you in difficulty, but to make you clean.'
(Surah 5:7.)

Women who are menstruating or have recently had babies are not supposed to touch the Qur'an.

Next, Muslims 'prepare the heart' by being aware of Allah's presence, and consciously thinking about Him. Even though they cannot see Allah, they know Allah can see them, for the Qur'an states:

'He is with you, wherever you are.'
(Surah 57:4.)

Muslims recommend that a special position is adopted while reading the Qur'an, so that they are instantly aware in their bodies that this is not just an ordinary book which they can read slumped in a chair. They often sit cross-legged on the floor with the Qur'an on a little rehl or wooden stand in front of them. Muslims never place the Qur'an on the floor.

The special position for reading is not compulsory, but Muslims try to train their bodies to respect the Qur'an, as well as their minds.

Naturally, Allah's enemy **Satan** will do everything possible to put Muslims off this study: he will create doubts, make them too busy, make them forget. This is why many Muslims start their reading with the verses:

'When you recite the Qur'an, seek refuge with Allah from Satan, the rejected one.'
(Surah 16:98.)

When not in use, the Qur'an is wrapped in a cloth to keep it free of dust, and it is usually placed on a high shelf in the room so that nothing is above it. Muslims would not put anything down on top of the Qur'an: it is treated with great respect.

NEW WORDS

Satan the force of evil opposed to Allah
Wudu ritual washing to bring a state of purity

FOR DISCUSSION

1 Explain how Muslims believe that tilawah is different from reading something like a novel or a magazine.

2 Why do you think Muslims take such care of their copies of the Qur'an?

3 If you had a special holy book, what arrangements would you make in your house for looking after it?

THINGS TO DO

1 Draw a picture, or a series of pictures, to illustrate the theme 'The Qur'an is always treated with respect'.

2 Copy out one of the sayings from the Qur'an in this unit and draw a border round it.

9 The listening Qur'an

This section tells you how Muslims believe that Allah is aware of you and listening to you, and that you should listen to Him.

Muslims always take for granted the idea that the message of the Qur'an is guidance for them as individuals, and not just a book of holy thoughts. It is a very personal message, and when it is read with faith, Muslims get the strong feeling that a real someone is listening to their particular problems, and is willing to help and support them. To achieve this awareness, Allah frequently adopts a direct method of heart-to-heart conversation in the Qur'an between Himself and all people.

The Muslim **shahadah**, or 'declaration of faith', states simply that 'There is no God but Allah, and Muhammad is the Prophet of God'. The first acceptance is the vital point: that there really is a God. This moment of realization is called **ihsan**. Realization is the heart of religion, and can begin even when faith – or even just the possibility of faith – is very weak. No religious leader or teacher in the world can make it happen, although they do their best to guide people towards God. Sometimes, because of the nature of human weakness and failure, the teacher's best is not good enough, is not convincing, or seems hypocritical. You cannot

Pilgrims on hajj. 'Here I am at Thy service, O Allah, ready to obey Thee.' (Pilgrim prayer.)

be forced to feel faith, any more than you can be forced to feel love. It is a matter of awareness. Those who become aware of the 'presence' of God realize that He sees everything and knows everything – even the number of hairs on their heads, and their innermost secret thoughts.

Reactions to hearing the Qur'an

Muslims with awareness have a great feeling of love, a kind of overwhelming joy and gratitude and amazement that Allah can see them and actually cares about them. He can see everything they have gone through, and loves them. Even when they felt most alone, they suddenly see that they were not alone at all, but that Allah was with them.

Muslims regard the Qur'an as the direct fulfilment of Allah's promises to Adam and his descendants:

'My guidance shall come to you, and whoever follows My guidance, no fear shall be on them, neither shall they grieve.'

(Surah 2:38.)

Muslims remember that they can know nothing of Allah without it being His will to reveal it; they therefore approach the Qur'an in a spirit of humility and dependence, trusting that He will open up their eyes and hearts. When they are touched, or moved, by something in the text, they are thankful and praise Him.

'All thanks and praise be to Allah Who has guided us to this; we should never have found guidance had Allah not willed it so.'

(Surah 7:43.)

'Our Lord! Let not our hearts swerve [from the truth] after You have guided us; bestow upon us Your grace, for surely You alone are the Bestower.'

(Surah 3:8.)

Muslims believe that when they hear the Qur'an they are hearing Allah Himself speaking to them. Many times, it certainly seems as if the words are addressed straight to the individual person, as if they were dealing just with that person alone. This experience can move people to tears, especially when the words come as an answer to something they have worried about.

'When they hear what has been sent down to the messenger, you see their eyes overflow with tears, because of what they recognize as the truth. They cry, "Our Lord! We believe!"'

(Surah 5:86.)

FOR DISCUSSION

1 Explain what makes Muslims think the Qur'an is a 'personal' message.

2 Why do you think some Muslims have cried when reading the Qur'an?

3 How do you think personal awareness of Allah can help people who are:
i depressed;
ii frightened;
iii under stress;
iv about to do something wrong?

THINGS TO DO

1 Make a list of changes you think a person might have to make in everyday life after receiving ihsan:
i at home;
ii at school;
iii out shopping.

NEW WORDS

Ihsan realizing for yourself that Allah exists

Shahadah declaring that you believe in Allah and His Prophet

This section tells you about the art of 'beautiful writing', or calligraphy.

The Bismillah means: 'In the name of Allah, the Compassionate, the Merciful'.

> 'The good word is a good tree with root firm and branches in heaven.' (Surah 14:24.)

Muslims have become famous for their calligraphy and manuscript illumination. These two skills centre upon the Qur'an, for Muslims wanted to find styles of writing worthy of the Holy Words. They wished to present them in the best possible way.

The Arabs, who were the original Muslims, had hardly taken any notice of writing skills before Muhammad received the Qur'an. They were typical of many wandering tribes-people: they were clever with words and loved learning and reciting fine poetry, but never 'stored' it in writing. They relied on highly developed memories. Each poet would transmit his or her verses to two people of the younger generation who could be trusted to pass them on in their turn to others. This same tradition was originally used and taken for granted by the Prophet when he began to receive his revelations.

However, Muslims – who respected the completed Qur'an as the Word of Allah – wanted to concentrate their full attention on not making a mistake over a single word or letter. They soon began to make efforts to write in a script worthy of the words. The style which quickly took over from all earlier ways of writing took its name from the Iraqi town of Kufah, which was one of the early centres of Islamic culture.

Artwork

At first, there was no colourful artwork on the text, for two main reasons. First, Muslims

The inscription on the vase reads: 'There is no God but Allah, and Muhammad is His Messenger'.

believed that it was wrong to make pictures of heavenly beings, or even human beings; and secondly, they did not want people to pay attention to pictures and decoration, rather than the writing itself. (The most beautiful artwork on special Qur'ans are designs and motifs which form a background to the text, or 'lead into' the opening letter.) Later, however, rich **sultans** commissioned artists to produce lavish and colourful Qur'ans, with the pages decorated in gold, green, red and blue. For example, the Ottoman Sultan Bayazid II valued the work of the master writer Hamd Allah al-Amasi so highly that he acted as his humble servant, holding the inkpot as he wrote, cutting his reed pens for him and mixing his ink from lamp black and vinegar.

The master writers believed in mysticism, and one of their beliefs was that handwriting revealed a person's inner character. So the perfect handwriting was held to be a sign of inward perfection and spirituality. Purity of writing showed purity of soul. The master calligraphers were, therefore, not just scribes, but deeply religious people. All the masters traced their 'spiritual art' back to the Prophet's son-in-law Ali, although there is some doubt as to whether he truly wrote a Qur'an himself in his own handwriting. Many Qur'ans are still written by hand, even though printing has been invented.

Islamic calligraphy is also used for decorating buildings, because of the disapproval of statues or pictures, and can be found on wall tiles, pottery, embroidery and wall carpets. In Muslim homes, instead of pictures or shelf ornaments, you can often see decorative Qur'anic texts in the shape of a mosque, or a 'ship of life', or some other intricate design.

NEW WORD

Sultan leader of a Muslim state

The ship of life. The 'boat' reads: 'I believe in Allah, and His angels, His books, His prophets, the Last Day, predestination, good and evil, and resurrection after death'. The 'sail' reads: 'There is no God but Allah and Muhammad is His messenger'.

FOR DISCUSSION

1 Why did the original Arab Muslims not pay much attention at first to writing the Qur'an down?

2 Why did calligraphers think that it was important for their writing to be both accurate and pure?

3 There was a recent outrage in the UK when a shoe was on sale with Qur'anic verses on it. Why do you think this annoyed Muslims so much?

THINGS TO DO

1 Here is a list of things that might be decorated with Qur'anic verses. Which of these would Muslims accept, and which would they reject? Explain why.

Wall picture; everyday cup; floor carpet; necklace; shoe; brooch; hanging for the car; special vase; chair cover; tablecloth.

2 Look at the Bismillah. Create your own design on a postcard or piece of art paper, and give it a beautiful geometric background decoration.

12 The unseen universe

This section tells you how Muslims believe that the Qur'an reveals aspects of Allah's creation that are unseen by human eyes.

Muslims believe that the only reason why Allah is not believed in by everybody is that He can only be 'seen' or understood according to His choice. To Muslims Allah is so great that He lies completely beyond the power of human understanding; people can only know about Him at all if He chooses to reveal something about Himself. (Notice the word 'He'; all the holy books call God 'He', although there is no evidence at all of God being male or female.)

The Qur'an states:

> 'No vision can grasp Him, but His grasp is over all vision: He is above all comprehension, yet He Himself knows everything.' (Surah 6:103.)

> 'There is no God but He, the Living, the Eternal. He neither slumbers nor sleeps. No person can grasp anything of His knowledge except as He wills it.' (Surah 2:255.)

The unseen world is known as **al-Ghaib**. The Qur'an suggests that the world we can see is only like the tip of an iceberg – there is far more in al-Ghaib than in our physical universe. For example, the human soul and its quest to return to the presence of Allah is part of al-Ghaib. The ultimate place where human souls will spend their eternities is also al-Ghaib. The person will either earn **paradise**, which the Qur'an frequently describes in terms of a beautiful garden where purity and love prevail; or **hell** – a place of torment and despair and regret. However, although both 'places' are described in human language in the Qur'an, Allah made it quite clear that real knowledge of these 'places' is far beyond human understanding – just as a caterpillar cannot understand what it is to be a butterfly, nor could you guess what the oak tree will be from the acorn.

'Woe to me! Would that I were mere dust.'
(Surah 78:40.)

> 'In paradise I prepare for the righteous believers what no eye has ever seen, no ear has ever heard, and what the deepest mind could never imagine.'
> (Surah 32:17 and Hadith.)

> 'The value of this world in comparison to the Hereafter is like a droplet in the ocean.'
> (Hadith.)

Muslims believe it is awareness of al-Ghaib that alters human lives, for without the knowledge that there is a life to come, there is no motivation for action. Without this knowledge, humans are taking the gamble of believing that good and evil people will all come to the same end: dust. Denial of life after death and **qiyamah** (the Day of Judgement) makes all other beliefs meaningless.

Muslims regard awareness of Allah as a precious gift. Faith in Allah is a mixture of knowledge and belief; things are accepted on trust, and are revealed by people of insight. The Muslim word for faith is **iman**.

Angels, evil spirits and jinn

The Qur'an presents Allah as Creator not only of this earth and its universe, but also of many other dimensions, or 'heavens', where there are creatures completely beyond our understanding. Some of these 'beings' can have an influence on this earth and on us; the Qur'an names three types: angels, evil spirits and jinn. Muslims take it as part of their faith that these beings really exist.

Angels are used by Allah as messengers and revealers in certain situations. They act as witnesses and warners to human beings, stirring their consciences when they are considering doing something wrong, giving premonitions of troubles to come, gathering with joy whenever humans pray or praise Allah, and recording all the good and bad deeds of individual humans in their 'book' – the record of their lives, on which their judgement will be based.

Muslims believe that evil spirits work actively to make people disbelieve in Allah, and go wrong. Jinns are creatures who live amongst humans, and they can be either good or evil. Although they are not usually seen, they can make people feel nervous in certain places, and sometimes upset people. Humans who have strong faith and love can deal with them by showing them a good

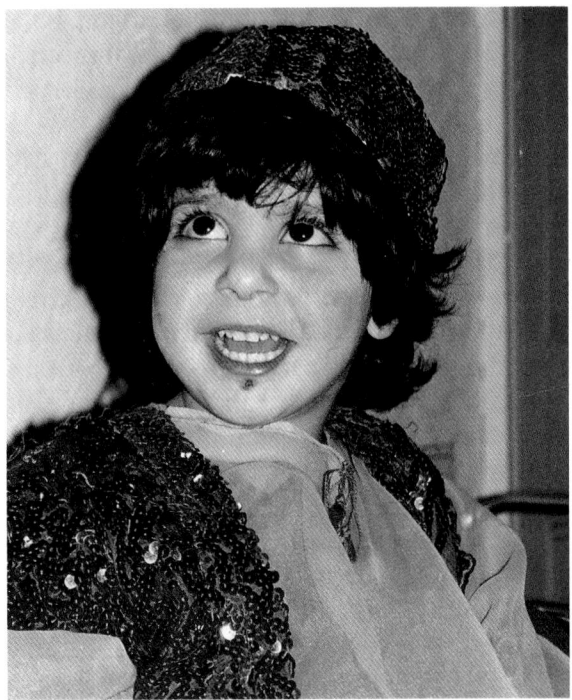

'Truly, for the righteous there will be a fulfilment of the heart's desire.' (Surah 78:31.)

example and influencing them to be good. The chief jinn is Shaytan (Satan), a being who opposes Allah and His human creations, and tries to make people do evil.

NEW WORDS

Al-Ghaib the unseen, the spiritual world

Hell the state of torment, the penalty for a bad life

Iman a person's faith

Paradise the state of bliss, the reward for a good life

Qiyamah the Day of Judgement

FOR DISCUSSION

1 Why do Muslims say it is impossible to 'know' or to 'see' Allah?

2 Why is awareness of al-Ghaib so important to the life of a believer?

3 Muslims take the existence of angels and jinn for granted. In what ways do you think jinn might try to frighten people, or tempt them to do evil? What do you think are the most important qualities a Muslim should have in order to deal with jinn?

THINGS TO DO

1 Make a list of some of the 'jobs' angels are supposed to do. Draw a series of pictures or cartoons to illustrate these jobs.

15 The saving message

'The believers, men and women, are protectors one of another.' (Surah 9:71.)

This section tells you how Muslims believe the Qur'an moves people to change their lives and bring them closer to Allah.

The Qur'an is intended to bring about changes. It tries to make people believe in Allah and live in a particular way. Once a person believes in Allah's ever-present reality, it alters every aspect of that person's life. The Qur'an therefore presents a complete way of life, and deals with every detail of it.

The Qur'an was given to humanity as a:

'guidance and a mercy for believers'
(Surah 10:57.)

It is not intended to make people miserable because they have to give everything up. Instead it will make people very happy, for its wisdom is worth more than any other treasures they might gain (see Surah 10:58).

The earnest effort to live in a way pleasing to Allah is called **jihad**, or 'striving'. This means putting Allah first in every situation; it means recognizing evil in its many forms, and fighting it. Sometimes Muslims get involved in military warfare and call this jihad – but real jihad is only war against evil on behalf of Allah, and has nothing to do with territory or nationalism. In fact, Muhammad despised nationalism, which he believed made people hate each other. He said: 'nationalism means supporting your people in unjust causes'; and 'he who proclaims the cause of nationalism is not one of us!'.

However, the world in which we live is full of troubles and sorrows, and also a lot of bad things which are attractive and lead us into mischief. Muslims call this world of physical attractions **dunya**. They believe that sometimes the enjoyable activities of dunya are real evils that corrupt and hurt and destroy

– like the lust for sex, or power, or greed for money, or the irresponsible use of drugs. Muslims regard these things as dangerous, because people are tempted by them.

The guide to life

The Qur'an is seen as one of the major weapons against the forces of darkness and evil, because it gives a very full and detailed guide of how one should live – what one should do, what one should avoid or give up, and what one should reject and fight. It points out clearly what Allah regards as wrongs and sins, and makes it quite clear that although humans have free will, if they choose to live in a wicked or selfish manner, they will have to face the consequences of their actions. Indeed, many Muslims believe that those who read the Qur'an but then choose not to act on its guidance are more likely to be cursed and punished than blessed:

'He is not a believer who makes **halal** what Allah has made **haram**.' (Hadith.)

It is regarded by Muslims as a real tragedy if someone reads the Qur'an and still goes away unmoved, or untouched. If there is no understanding, and no action following it to improve a person's life, then the readers are regarded as '...like a donkey carrying books' (Surah 62:5), taking the weight of them, but gaining no understanding or benefit.

The saving message

One of the most important aspects of the Qur'an, that has real practical benefit in 'saving' people, is its message of hope and confidence. When things go wrong, or when tragedies strike, many people wonder why it has happened to them or their loved ones, and they give up belief in God and become terribly depressed. Muslims believe it would hardly be reasonable for Allah to place people in situations which are too much for them, and then expect them to be successful. That would make Him very unfair. Instead, the Qur'an promises that:

'...on no soul does Allah place a burden greater than it can bear.' (Surah 2:286; 23:62.)

Therefore, Muslims believe we should never give up in despair, even though we may think things are unbearable at the time we are going through them. We should cling on to hope and faith.

FOR DISCUSSION

1 Explain the real meaning of jihad for Muslims in everyday life. How could a Muslim carry out jihad both in the home and at school?

2 Why do you think Muhammad was so much against nationalism?

3 Why do you think Muslims believe Allah might punish people who had read the guidance but not acted on it?

THINGS TO DO

1 Which of these statements are true according to Muslims, and which are false? Copy out any statements which Muslims consider to be true; alter the others to fit in with the Muslim beliefs.
   i The Qur'an only applies to certain parts of life.
   ii The urges for power, sex and money don't need to be controlled.
   iii Allah forces people to believe in Him.
   iv Allah promises that no test should be too much for us.

2 Make a list of 'attractive' things that might make people go wrong in life – the things which Muslims call dunya. Explain why Muslims think Allah is against these things.

NEW WORDS

Dunya the attractive things of this world

Halal things which are permitted or allowed

Haram things which are forbidden

Jihad striving one's hardest to please Allah

16 The consistent and final Qur'an

This section tells you that the Qur'an always agrees with itself; there are no 'puzzles'. It is complete and final.

If Muhammad had been a learned scholar, who had studied books and could write fluently, then people who do not believe in the Qur'an would have a fair point when they suggest that it could all have come from the hand and mind of Muhammad himself. However, Muhammad lived at a brutish and selfish time, when people were steeped in ignorance and **superstition**. The greatest ideas of people at that time were confined to their limited surroundings. Even the great scholars lacked the sort of everyday knowledge possessed by ordinary people today.

Consistency

Muslims maintain that the Qur'an carries its own proof of divine authorship, because if you study it from any angle, its message is entirely consistent, although it was surely impossible for any human author to remain consistent in everything he was teaching for a period of 23 years! Although the surahs of the Qur'an are not in the order in which they were revealed, and were given over so long a time, there are no compromises and no contradictions.

A beautiful modern mosque in Jeddah.

'Do they not consider the Qur'an with care? Had it been from other than Allah, they would surely have found many discrepancies in it.'

(Surah 4:82.)

Sometimes, as the years went by, Allah returned to the same subject and added further words. In these cases:

'Say – Whenever He suppresses a verse, or causes it to be forgotten, We bring one which is better or similar. Do you not know that Allah can do anything?' (Surah 2:106.)

This is highly remarkable when you realize that a lot of the things mentioned in the Qur'an were not known even to the men of science of Muhammad's time – there were all sorts of wild speculations about the universe, and plenty of myths and legends which had been put over by people in authority as 'truth'. If the Qur'an had all come from the mind of Muhammad, then there was plenty of chance for him to make mistakes, and contradict himself.

Every time Muhammad was asked to give a sign or proof, he pointed straight away to the revealed words. They themselves were the proof; they did not need any other support. If a thing was true, it would soon be seen to be true. It would be self-evident.

'Truth stands out clear from error.'

(Surah 2:256.)

Finding answers

Whatever question or problem might be troubling anyone, they could look into the Qur'an and find either the answer or the principle by which the answer could be deduced – and it would be there. The answer might not always be what a weak or conceited or selfish or greedy person might hope to find, for they would be looking for some way of justifying the wrong things they were doing – but the answer would be there, and it would be clear and just. Any person who then

rejected that answer would deliberately be choosing to go against reason and justice.

'Nay, here are signs self-evident in the hearts of those endowed with knowledge. And none but the unjust reject our signs.'

(Surah 29:49.)

The seal of the prophets

Muslims believe that Muhammad was to be the last prophet, the seal of all the messengers that went before, and that no further prophets would be necessary. The Qur'an – studied alongside a knowledge of Muhammad's way of life and example, and using Islamic principles of deduction and reason when applying it to a 'modern' problem – is seen as a complete revelation, final for all time.

FOR DISCUSSION

1 Why do Muslims claim that the fact that the Qur'an is consistent with itself is a proof of its divine authorship?

2 Why do Muslims call the Blessed Muhammad the 'seal' of the prophets?

THINGS TO DO

1 Choose one of the sayings from the Qur'an and copy it out with a decorative border.

2 Make a list of things that you think would go against the 'character' of Allah, as understood by Muslims. For example: if Allah is true, it would be impossible for Him to tell a lie, make an incorrect statement about science – and so on.

NEW WORD

Superstition belief in luck, magic and things which are not there

17 The scientific message

This section tells you how Muslims believe that the message of the Qur'an is always consistent with modern scientific discovery.

The Qur'an is not intended to be a textbook of scientific knowledge, and it has little to say about specific scientific matters. However, Muslims believe that what it does say is always totally consistent with modern knowledge about the universe, although the people of Muhammad's time were highly superstitious, and many worshipped the sun, moon and stars as if they were personalities. There is no such mythology or superstition in the Qur'an.

> 'They ask you concerning the new moons. Say: they are but signs to mark fixed periods of time.' (Surah 2:189.)

The immensity of space.

In fact, although no scientist knows the real truths of the universe to this day, the Qur'an gives some revelations that are quite consistent with the theories of the big bang and the expanding universe.

> 'Do not the unbelievers see that the heavens and the earth were joined together [as one unit of creation] before We clove them asunder? ... And it is He Who created the night and the day, the sun and the moon, all [the celestial bodies] swim along, each in its set orbit.' (Surah 21:30,33.)

When were all these things discovered? Only very recently. We now know that the sun is a star so huge that 1.3 million earths could fit inside it. It is 93 million miles away from us. Yet if you put the star Betelgeuse where the sun is, it would swallow us up and reach right up to the planet Jupiter! Whatever 'banged', it was a very big bang!

Our galaxy, the Milky Way, has over 100 billion stars in it – and Muslims believe that nothing in it is the chaotic product of random or chance forces. Our brains cannot begin to grasp the immensity of these collections of stars, or the vast distances involved. Is it

possible that an uneducated Arab over 1,400 years ago could have known these things?

Life on earth

What about the origin of life on earth? Billions of years ago, primeval matter in the sea began to form living things. When was this discovered? Again, only very recently. Yet the Qur'an states:

> 'And We made from water every living thing. Will they then not believe?' (Surah 21:30.)

> 'Allah has created every animal from water; some [of these creatures now] creep on their bellies, some walk on two legs and some on four. Allah creates what He wills, for truly He has power over all things.' (Surah 24:45.)

And what about the other end of the scale? There are many living things so minute that no human eye has ever seen them. All adult humans, with all their physical characteristics, were once no more than a minute 'computer programme' in a living cell. Muslims believe that Adam and Eve were real, created people, and that both male and female came from the same original soul, which divided.

'O humanity – remember your duty to Allah, Who created you from a single soul, and from it created its mate, and from the two created many men and women.' (Surah 4:1.)

Once Allah had created the principle of male and female pairs, reproduction by sex instead of cell-division became possible.

Botanists, zoologists, physicists and chemists can all find modern truths in the Qur'an. Muslims believe this is all part of the miraculous nature of the revelations, for when these particular parts of the message were revealed, 1,400 years ago, the scientific details were meaningless. In fact, modern Muslim scientists claim they were really addressed to today's Muslims!

What about the end of the world? Once again, there is no man-made mythology or speculation in the Qur'an:

'Say: Knowledge of this is with Allah alone; none but He can reveal when it will occur...all of a sudden it will come to you.' (Surah 7:187.)

FOR DISCUSSION

1 How was the science of the Qur'an different from the thoughts and mythologies of Muhammad's time?

2 Why do Muslims regard the scientific understanding in the Qur'an as being miraculous?

THINGS TO DO

1 Muslims do not believe in chance or accident, but in a Supreme Creator, who plans even individual humans. Make a list of some of the things that might have been present in your 'computer programme' before you were born: for example, skin colour, special features, talents and abilities.

2 Draw a picture to illustrate the idea of the 'big bang' or the 'expanding universe', or the planets in their orbits. Write a few sentences to describe the Muslim idea of the greatness of Allah the Creator.

'Eye has not seen and it has not entered into the human heart what things Allah has prepared for those that love Him.' (Hadith Muslim.)

18 Hadith and sunnah

This section tells you about the authority of the Prophet Muhammad and the significance of his life and sayings for Muslims.

> 'O Prophet! Truly We have sent you as a witness, a bearer of good news, and a warner – as one who invites to Allah's [grace] by His leave, and as a lamp spreading light.'
>
> (Surah 33:45–46.)

To have real understanding of the Qur'an it is necessary to move as close as possible to the Prophet who was its messenger. The whole life of the Blessed Muhammad is regarded by Muslims as a 'living Qur'an'. If you wish to study the Qur'an in action, you have to study the Prophet and all his deeds and sayings. As his beloved third wife Aisha said of him: 'His way of life is the Qur'an'.

The hadith

Every act and detail of the Blessed Muhammad's life was of the greatest interest to those around him because of his unique position as chosen Messenger of Allah. Muhammad's deeds and sayings are known as hadiths, and they run into many thousands.

The true hadiths were recorded and preserved by those who knew Muhammad very well. In later times it became much more difficult to know whether a hadith was genuine or not, and scholars always look carefully to see who remembered it, and where that person got it from.

The truth and accuracy of hadiths is a matter of vital importance, because they deal with all aspects of putting the Qur'an into practice,

from the most personal and intimate matters to the conduct of war and affairs of state.

Sometimes statements in the Qur'an are very brief, or not very clear or detailed. Muhammad's life and teachings supplied all the details of the Muslim 'way': they supplemented and explained the Qur'an, and made clear anything that was not clear in it.

For example, the Qur'an recommends prayer during the night over and above the five compulsory prayers:

> 'Celebrate the praises of your Lord before the rising of the sun and before its setting; yea, celebrate them for part of the hours of the night, and at the sides of the day, that you may have spiritual joy.'   (Surah 68:130.)

Prayer positions follow the sunnah of the Prophet. 'Be steadfast in prayer... for God sees well all that you do.'
(Surah 2:110.)

Although Muhammad himself prayed every night, he knew Allah understood human weaknesses, and taught that extremism and forcing oneself to suffer was not necessary:

'When one of you dozes in prayer, he should sleep until his sleep is gone.'
(Hadith Abu Dawud – recorded by Aisha.)

'When one of you gets up at night to pray and falters in reciting the Qur'an, and does not understand what he utters, he should sleep.'
(Hadith Abu Dawud – recorded by Abu Hurairah.)

'Any person who regularly prays at night, but on a certain night is defeated by sleep, he will still be given the reward for it (by God) as if he did pray.'
(Hadith Abu Dawud – recorded by Aisha.)

An account of the Prophet's life is known as a **sirah**, a 'path' or 'way'. The earliest known sirah of the Prophet is by Ibn Hisham. A shortened version of this, by Ibn Ishaq, has been translated into English.

The example of the right way of life given by Muhammad is known as the **sunnah**. The Qur'an and the sunnah together form the guidance for Muslim lives. From these two things Muslim law-codes were compiled by eminent scholars. These codes of conduct are known as the **shariah**, another word meaning 'path'.

Muhammad's authority

Some Muslims feel that the sunnah cannot be considered equal to the Qur'an itself; they take the view that if Allah had particularly wished anything to be a part of Islam, it would have been revealed in the Qur'an. Against this, however, most Muslims point out the authority given to Muhammad by the Qur'an itself, and argue that Allah obviously intended the Prophet's sunnah to be taken as the 'living example' of His wishes carried into action.

'It is not fitting for a believer, man or woman, when a matter has been decided by Allah and His Messenger, to have any option about their decision; if anyone disobeys Allah and His Messenger, he [or she] is indeed on a path that is clearly wrong.'   (Surah 33:36.)

How do Muslims know Muhammad was a genuine Prophet of Allah? The fact is, they don't. This is why the second part of the Muslim statement of faith, the shahadah, is also an act of faith. Muslims are declaring that they believe totally in the genuine prophetic calling of Muhammad, and that the message revealed through him by the **Ummul Kitab** (the 'Mother of Books') and his way of life replaced everything that Allah had revealed to humanity before.

NEW WORDS

Shariah the 'way' of the Prophet; Islamic law

Sirah the life of the Prophet

Sunnah the example given by Muhammad's life and practices

Ummul Kitab 'Mother of Books'; 'mother of' is an Arabic expression meaning 'the greatest of'

FOR DISCUSSION

1 Why do you think Aisha said of Muhammad 'His way of life is the Qur'an'? What did she mean?

2 Why are the hadiths and sunnah so important to Muslims?

THINGS TO DO

1 Write a short dialogue or debate between two people. One should be a Muslim who believes the hadiths are as important as the Qur'an, and the other should be someone who thinks the hadiths may not be reliable.

19 The Prophet's 'way'

This section tells you something about the Prophet's example, and his way of life that was the 'living Qur'an'.

Muhammad was not a super-human being. He was a man like other men, subject to the same strengths and weaknesses, and tempted by the same temptations. He lived an extremely full, active and complete life. He was a devoted husband, father and grandfather, a faithful friend, a noble leader both in worship and on the battlefield, and a famous and influential statesman.

Muslims love Muhammad because his life was so completely submitted to the way of Allah, as laid down in the Qur'an, that he became the True Guide in every situation. He did not withdraw to a special religious or protected community, but lived amongst the people for whom the guidance was intended, showing how it worked in practice. He was expected by Allah to serve as a living example, and this is how his way of life helped (and still helps) other Muslims.

To this day, if Muslims have a problem for which they cannot find an answer in the Qur'an, they study the hadith to see if Muhammad ever faced a similar problem, and to find out how he coped with it. For Muslims, he is the model, the teacher and guide, and he is loved, revered and copied above all other men.

> 'You have indeed in the Apostle of Allah a beautiful pattern – for anyone whose hope is in Allah and the Final Day, and who praises Allah.'   (Surah 33:21.)

Moderation

Two of the most important aspects of his sunnah were gentleness and moderation. Muhammad always advised people to avoid extremes and to try to gain a balanced outlook on life. He disapproved of an over-proud fanaticism just as much as a lazy, couldn't-care-less attitude. Even though he was highly spiritual himself, he knew that Allah did not order religious people to abandon the world,

or give up all comfort and put themselves through inconvenience and self-denial in a life devoted to prayer. If they did this, there was always a danger it would make them so fanatical that they would neglect the humans they were called upon to love. At least once he reprimanded a husband for spending too much time praying at the mosque and making his neglected wife unhappy. Another time he rebuked a wife who fasted too often, and deprived her husband of his marital pleasures.

However, Muhammad believed firmly that Muslims should control their passions, and not let any part of their personalities take control over them. They were to seek peace and happiness, but not at the expense of others, or in ways that harmed others.

Muhammad's example

Muhammad was always especially kind to the poor, to children, to slaves and to women – to those who usually suffered. He was also extremely kind to animals, and thoughtful about all forms of life.

'Accept what Allah gives you, and you will be the richest of all people.' (Hadith Tirmidhi.)

'Some people recite Qur'an, but it does not go down beyond their collarbones. It is beneficial only when it settles in the heart, and is rooted deeply in it.' (Hadith Muslim.)

One hadith of Muhammad's friend Anas showed his consideration and lack of fanaticism. He said of his public prayer services:

'I never prayed behind an Imam who was more brief or more perfect in his prayer than Allah's messenger. If he heard a baby cry he would shorten his prayer for fear that the mother might be distressed.'

People's private prayers could go on as long as they liked.

Muhammad believed strongly in good manners – always greeting people kindly, showing respect to elders, and balancing his serious teachings with gentle good humour:

'The dearest of you to me are those who have good manners; the most offensive to me are the most boring and the long-winded!'

If anyone had been unpleasant to him, he always behaved pleasantly back, and forgave them:

'Allah will not show mercy to him who does not show mercy to others.'

'Don't tell me anything unpleasant concerning another, for I wish when I meet that person to have my mind unbiased.'

Muhammad was never arrogant or 'superior'. He always behaved simply, despite his eminent position as leader, making no-one feel small, unwanted or embarrassed. People who sat in his company never felt that he was rude to them, or that he ignored or neglected them. He never turned his face away from the person he was talking to. He never acted in a superior manner to slaves, but always treated them with respect, calling them 'my son' or 'my daughter'. He disliked snobbery and pride, and anything that divided people and stopped them feeling as if they were all Allah's 'family'.

FOR DISCUSSION

1 Why is the Prophet's example of moderation and understanding so important to Muslims?

2 How is it possible that a Muslim man wishing to improve his spirituality by spending the longest possible time at the mosque might be earning de-merit rather than merit for his way of life?

THINGS TO DO

1 Imagine you are one of the young Muslims of Madinah. Write a letter to a friend explaining why it is important to you that Muhammad lived an 'ordinary' life, facing the same temptations as everybody else.

20 The discipline of the Qur'an

This section tells you about the **five pillars** of Islam, requested in the Qur'an and outlined in detail by Muhammad.

Although the Qur'an makes it very clear that nobody can be forced to be religious –

> 'Let there be no compulsion in religion'
> (Surah 2:256.)

– nevertheless, there are five acts of discipline that Muhammad highlighted in his last great public sermon which are now regarded as compulsory for all Muslims. These are known as the five pillars of the faith, because they hold up the entire 'building' which is Islam.

The first of these pillars is shahadah, or the act of bearing witness. Every Muslim, before he or she can claim to be Muslim, has to acknowledge in the heart and in public the belief that Allah really exists, and the acceptance that Muhammad was Allah's genuine prophet. After this, it is the Muslim's duty to pass this knowledge on to others.

> 'It is Allah Who has named you Muslims, both before and in this revelation; that the Messenger [Muhammad] may be a witness for you, and you be witnesses for all humanity.' (Surah 22:78.)

The next two 'pillars' are **salah**, the practice of special regular prayers, and **zakah**, a tax on wealth.

> 'Those who believe, and do deeds of righteousness, and establish regular prayers and regular giving, will have their reward with their Lord; on them shall be no fear, nor shall they grieve.' (Surah 2:277.)

The words said in salah, and the actions to be performed, were not given in the Qur'an. They are part of the sunnah, the example laid down by the Prophet. The Qur'an states:

> **'Spend from your substance out of love for Him.'**
> **(Surah 2:177.)**

> 'Celebrate the praises of our Lord before the rising of the sun and before its setting; yes, celebrate them for part of the watches of the night, and at the sides of the day, that you may have spiritual joy.'
> (Surah 20:130; see also 11:114; 17:78–79; 30:17–18 – 'Give glory to Allah when you reach eventide and when you rise in the morning.')

The particular way that Muslims pray – in lines shoulder to shoulder, standing to attention with the hands near the ears, then bending over, then going down on the knees and touching the forehead, nose, hands, knees and toes to the earth – was a set routine taught by Muhammad as part of his sunnah.

If Muslims wish to say other prayers – and many Muslims have a prayerful awareness of Allah throughout all the moments of the day – these are known as **du'a'**, or personal prayers. When Muslims are praying together in the mosque, there obviously have to be set times to begin, and most mosques now provide a printed timetable. Elsewhere, Muslims can be less precise, as long as the prayer is made between the stated times.

Zakah is the duty of paying regard to one's income, and finding something to spare for the less fortunate. Muslims must:

'...spend of your substance out of love for Him, for your family, for orphans, for the needy, for the wayfarer (or refugee), for those who have need, and for the freeing of slaves.' (Surah 2:177.)

It is not just a matter of personal charity or emotion. After Muslims have provided sensibly for themselves and dependents, they have to give a 40th of any surplus away. This is not a great burden for most people, but it teaches them to think and care for others. In the end, they will not lose by it, for:

'Whatever you spend in charity or devotion, be sure Allah knows it all.' (Surah 2:270.)

'Ramadan is the month in which the Qur'an was set down... so every one of you... should spend it in fasting.' (Surah 2:185.)

The next pillar is **saum**, or fasting. The fast starts at first light. Nothing must enter the body until after sunset – no food, drink or cigarettes. All sexual activity also waits, and such things as medicine and injections, if possible – but people who would become ill without them are excused the fast. It is quite a severe test – while it is a month of self-denial, it is also a time of satisfaction and joy. Families and friends draw especially close. Muhammad emphasized the correct attitude:

'If you cannot give up hatred and enmity, there is no need to give up food and drink.' (Hadith.)

The final pillar is to:

'make the **hajj** ... in the service of Allah.' (Surah 2:196.)

All Muslims have to try to get to Makkah (if they can afford it, and nobody else would be made to suffer if they went), once in their lifetime, during the special week which ends with **Eid ul Adha**. Some Muslims go often – but now the numbers of pilgrims are so vast that this is no longer regarded as a good thing. Those who wish to go for extra visits can go during other times of the year, when the pilgrimage is known as **umrah**. During hajj, there are often over a million pilgrims.

Muslims who make hajj often say it is the high spot of their lives. It is a very moving experience to be part of a vast throng, and yet to feel that Allah has seen and noticed you, accepted your sacrifice and forgiven your sins.

FOR DISCUSSION

1 Explain why total commitment to Allah has to come before Muslims can attend to the other pillars in their daily lives.

2 Why do you think most Muslims love keeping the 'five pillars', and do not regard them as a burden? What do you think they get out of it?

THINGS TO DO

1 Draw a series of pictures or diagrams to illustrate each of the five pillars. You could make these into a poster.

2 Imagine you are a Muslim. Choose one of the pillars, and list what you would have to do in order to get ready to fulfil it, and how you would go about it.

NEW WORDS

Du'a' private and personal prayers

Eid ul Adha the feast of sacrifice during hajj

Five pillars the five religious disciplines of Islam

Hajj pilgrimage to Makkah two months after Ramadan

Salah ritual prayer with set movements and words

Saum fasting during the hours of daylight

Umrah pilgrimage to Makkah at any time of year other than two months after Ramadan

Zakah tax on income

21 The practical message

This section tells you about the practical way of life required for Muslims by the Qur'an and demonstrated by Muhammad's example.

Allah requires His followers to treat everybody generously, kindly, honestly, truthfully, fairly and courteously. One particular passage makes this very clear, and is like a summary of Islam:

> 'It is not righteousness that you turn your faces towards East or West; but it is righteousness to believe in Allah and the Last Day, and the angels, the Book and the messengers; to spend out of your substance out of love for Him, for your family, for orphans, for the needy, for the wayfarer (and the refugee), for those who ask, and for the freeing of slaves; to be steadfast in prayer and give regular charity, to fulfil the contracts you have made, and to be firm and patient when in suffering and adversity, and throughout all period of panic. Such are the people of truth, the God-fearing.'
>
> (Surah 2:177.)

The Prophet showed, by his generous and humble way of life, that this was indeed the way to live. Believers should take care of each other's feelings, avoid indecent and abusive language and manners, help each other, attend to the sick, support the destitute, assist the needy, try to find work for the unemployed and sympathize with all those stricken by trouble.

> 'Visit the sick, feed the hungry and release the suffering.'   (Hadith.)

The hadiths present a very clear picture of the Prophet's deep concern for people. He knew how to guide them and motivate them, and appeal to their better natures. He gave realistic advice, and when he had to be stern, he did it gently. He never taught by words alone, but his example always put his words into practice. Even when he became a head of state, Muhammad always lived very simply, and gave away the wealth that was donated to him. He did not believe that wealthy Muslims should ever squander upon themselves that which could maintain thousands of others:

> 'Two wolves let loose among a flock of sheep do not cause more damage than a person's greed for wealth.'

Breaking the fast after Ramadan.

Muhammad used to sleep on the floor on a simple rush mattress. He ate very simple food, often uncooked, and it was his practice never to leave the table with a full stomach. His simplicity was no barrier to his hospitality, however. Muhammad said:

> 'He is not a believer who eats his fill while his neighbour remains hungry by his side.'
> (Hadith.)

Muhammad loved Allah's world and believed that Allah had provided all the means and resources to fulfil all the needs of humanity – if only people did not waste and misuse them. He said:

> 'The world is green and beautiful, and Allah has appointed you His stewards over it.'
> (Hadith.)

Muhammad taught that any misuse was wrong. This applied whether it was something that would harm the abuser (such as alcohol or drugs), harmed others or made the abuser unpleasant to others (such as theft or sexual abuse), or something that wasted the earth's resources, or spoilt them for nothing, or destroyed them. He believed that men and women should be modest and unassuming, not proud and arrogant. They should dress modestly, and not seek to attract attention to themselves:

> 'Modesty and faith are closely linked together; if either of them is lost, the other goes too.'
> (Hadith.)

He realized that people were often judged by others, especially by those who considered themselves to be very religious. Muhammad pointed out that:

> 'Allah does not look upon your outward appearance; He looks upon your hearts and your deeds.'
> (Hadith.)

If people made mistakes, it was important to keep them trying, not to drive them away. Muhammad taught the generosity of Allah:

> 'Make things easy, and do not make them hard; cheer people up, and do not rebuff them!'
> (Hadith.)

Muslims believe that the most beautiful aspect of Muhammad's teachings is his love and compassion – putting the will of the Compassionate One into practice. In simple words:

> 'You will not enter paradise until you have faith; and you cannot have faith until you love one another.'
> (Hadith.)

FOR DISCUSSION

1 How do the sayings and example of Muhammad reach the heart of Islam?

2 Which examples from the sayings and way of life of Muhammad would convince you that he was a genuine 'man of God', worthy of love and respect?

THINGS TO DO

1 Muslims regard as corrupt those authorities that have money which could be used to help deprived people but who just fritter it away in useless or extravagant decorations, palaces, exhibitions, fireworks, etc. Which of the following things would be regarded as Islamic or unIslamic? Divide the items into two separate lists.

   sewage works   fireworks display
   new hospital   new roads   golden dome on
   mosque   private rose garden   public park
   trade exhibition   new school   library
   expensive decoration of school or hospital

2 Make a list of words which you might use to describe the character of Muhammad.

22 The use of the Qur'an

In this section an **Imam**, Rahmat Aziz Salik, at the Hull Mosque, tells you how Muslims use the Qur'an in their daily lives.

'Follow that which comes to you by inspiration from your Lord.' (Surah 33:2.)

Interviewer: Imam, first tell us about your job. What sort of things do you do?

Imam: Firstly, I lead the five daily prayers, and the communal prayer on Fridays. I teach the children every day for two hours, Monday to Friday, and I teach adults for one hour on three days. Apart from that, I have to try to give guidance and help to my community, solving arguments, helping with housing problems and so on.

Interviewer: Imam, when and how is the Qur'an used in Muslim life?

Imam: The main use of the Qur'an is in the daily prayers and readings, but there are certain times when the Qur'an is especially treasured and recited. Most important is during the month of Ramadan, our annual

fast. The Qur'an is divided into 30 sections, which we read through, and we do special prayers called tarawih (or sunnah) prayers, with 20 **rakahs**, between 8pm and midnight each night, so that the whole Qur'an gets read through. In fact, if you go to the mosque at any time during Ramadan, you will find someone there reading the Qur'an. It goes on 24 hours a day.

Interviewer: Why is that?

Imam: The Qur'an was first given during this month, so it is regarded as especially holy. Many Muslims make it their business to recite the whole Qur'an during this month. Some of them withdraw altogether from normal life, and go into seclusion for a few days, or even all of the last ten days of Ramadan, and do nothing but read the Qur'an and pray for the whole community. They stay in the mosque, and take their food there.

Interviewer: Isn't there one special night in Ramadan?

Imam: It is said in surah 97 that the whole Qur'an descended from heaven on Lailat ul Qadr, the Night of Power. It came from the timelessness of Allah into the physical world of time and space when the Prophet was given the first verses of it. Nobody knows the exact day, but it is celebrated on one of the odd-numbered nights during the last ten days of Ramadan. All mosques remain full during this night, as the whole night is spent in prayer and reading the Qur'an. Just before dawn, they take breakfast, then make the dawn prayer (the fajr prayer), and then go to sleep after sunrise. Many of them sleep in the mosque. Some devout worshippers keep all five odd-numbered nights.

Interviewer: Is this only men?

Imam: Only men sleep at the mosque. Of course, women can also do the seclusion, but they do it in their own homes.

Interviewer: When else is the Qur'an read?

Imam: The one family occasion when the Qur'an is read right through aloud is when a loved one dies. Relatives and friends gather to take part in this reading. Sometimes they take it in turns; sometimes several people read different passages at the same time. When it is finished, they pray to Allah to bless the soul of the departed person.

Interviewer: Don't they also use the Qur'an for healing?

Imam: Yes. Sometimes Muslims use the Qur'an for 'practical' purposes, such as helping people who are suffering from physical or nervous illness, or who feel they are being afflicted by a jinn. The Prophet used to pray with sufferers and recite the Qur'an to them.

Interviewer: I've heard that sometimes devout but simple people carry miniature Qur'ans, or little pieces of script in a locket, believing they will help them like magic.

Imam: This is not really approved of. But sometimes if I am praying for a sick person, I read certain surahs seven times, then I blow on some water, and the sick one drinks it. It helps them.

'For those who believe and work righteous deeds is a reward that will never fail.' (Surah 41:8.)

Interviewer: What about using the Qur'an as jewellery?

Imam: Wearing miniature Qur'ans as jewellery or decoration is not really approved of, especially if one was to go into a toilet wearing them. Mind you, ladies' lockets are not real Qur'ans, but just little baubles of gold. Anyway, they usually have them on a long chain, so that they can easily be slipped off.

Interviewer: Do you have a favourite passage in the Qur'an?

Imam: Yes: Surah Ya-Sin. The Prophet said that 'every human being has a heart, and the heart of the Qur'an is Ya-Sin.' I read it every morning, and I feel peaceful and happy until sunset; it seems to make my day go smoothly:

'It would not be reasonable in me if I did not serve Him Who created me and to Whom shall you all be brought back.' (Surah 36:22.)

FOR DISCUSSION

1 Explain why the month of Ramadan is so special for the Qur'an.

THINGS TO DO

1 Imagine you are a visitor to the mosque on one of the odd-numbered nights at the end of Ramadan. Describe what you might see there, and explain why this is going on.

2 Imagine you are the Imam of a mosque in your area. Make a diary for your day's events, showing how you give time to prayers, teaching and helping people.

NEW WORDS

Imam a respected person who guides the Muslim community

Rakahs units of prayer, the full cycle of standing, bowing and kneeling positions

Glossary

Al-Ghaib the unseen, the spiritual world

Persecution being hurt or ridiculed by other people

Prophet a person who receives a message from God

Qiyamah the Day of Judgement religion

Du'a' private and personal prayers

Dunya the attractive things of this world

Eid ul Adha the feast of sacrifice during hajj

Five pillars the five religious disciplines of Islam

Hadith a saying or teaching of Muhammad's own

Hafiz someone who has learnt the whole Qur'an by heart

Hajj pilgrimage to Makkah two months after Ramadan

Halal things which are permitted or allowed

Haram things which are forbidden

Hell the state of torment, the penalty for a bad life

Ihsan realizing for yourself that Allah exists

Imam a respected person who guides the Muslim community

Iman a person's faith

Islam the religion of 'submission to Allah (God)'

Jihad striving one's hardest to please Allah

Jinn a kind of being, either good or evil, created by God

Lailat ul-Miraj the night Muhammad had his special 'journey' to heaven

Lailat ul Qadr the Night of Power: the night when Muhammad first received a revelation from Allah

Missionary somebody sent out by God to do His work and tell people about Him

Paradise the state of bliss, the reward for a good life

Persecution being hurt or ridiculed by other people

Prophet a person who receives a message from God

Qayamah the Day of Judgement

Rakahs units of prayer, the full cycle of standing, bowing and kneeling positions

Revelation a message sent from God to a human mind

Sacrifice giving something to God (usually the life of an animal) or going without something you value for the sake of God

Salah ritual prayer with set movements and words

Satan the force of evil opposed to Allah

Saum fasting during the hours of daylight

Shahadah declaring that you believe in Allah and His Prophet

Shariah the 'way' of the Prophet; Islamic law

Shirk a belief that Allah's power or Person can be divided

Sirah the life of the Prophet

Submission replacing your own will with someone else's

Sultan leader of a Muslim state

Sunnah the example given by Muhammad's life and practice

Superstition belief in luck, magic and things which are not there

Surah a section of the Qur'an organized as a chapter

Tawhid the unity and oneness of Allah

Ummul Kitab 'Mother of Books'; 'mother of' is an Arabic expression meaning 'the greatest of'

Umrah pilgrimage to Makkah at any time of year other than two months after Ramadan

Wudu ritual washing to bring a state of purity

Zakah Muslim tax on income